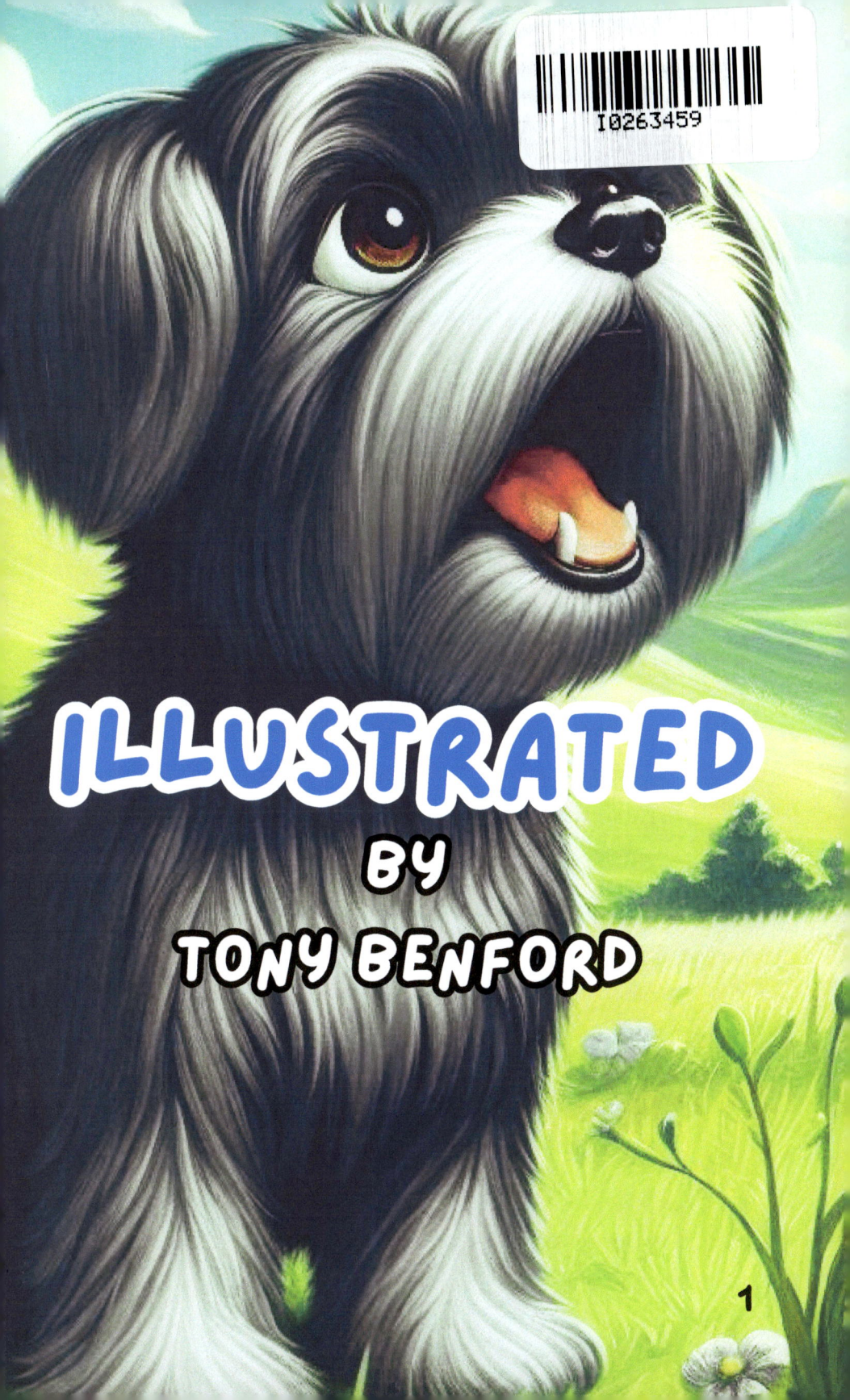

COPYRIGHT

COPYRIGHT © 2025 TONY BENFORD
ALL RIGHTS RESERVED.

NO PART OF THIS PUBLICATION MAY BE REPRODUCED, STORED IN A RETRIEVAL SYSTEM, OR TRANSMITTED IN ANY FORM OR BY ANY MEANS—ELECTRONIC, MECHANICAL, PHOTOCOPYING, RECORDING, OR OTHERWISE—WITHOUT THE PRIOR WRITTEN PERMISSION OF THE AUTHOR, EXCEPT IN THE CASE OF BRIEF QUOTATIONS EMBODIED IN CRITICAL ARTICLES OR REVIEWS.

WHERE'S DUKE? IS A WORK OF CREATIVE STORYTELLING INSPIRED BY BIBLICAL TRUTHS. WHILE SOME ELEMENTS ARE FICTIONALIZED FOR IMAGINATIVE PURPOSES, THE HEART OF THIS BOOK IS TO GLORIFY GOD AND INSPIRE FAITH IN READERS OF ALL AGES.

SCRIPTURE REFERENCES, UNLESS OTHERWISE NOTED, ARE TAKEN FROM THE NEW KING JAMES VERSION®, AND ARE USED BY PERMISSION.

COVER DESIGN AND ILLUSTRATIONS BY TONY BENFORD.

INDEPENDENTLY PUBLISHED BY THIRTY THREE & THREE PUBLISHING, LLC.

FIRST EDITION, 2025

FOR INQUIRIES OR PERMISSIONS, CONTACT:
THIRTYTHREEANDTHREE333@GMAIL.COM

NOTE FROM THE AUTHOR

DEAR READER,

IF YOU HAVE A FURRY FAMILY MEMBER, YOU KNOW THEIR AMAZING PERSONALITY, HOW SPECIAL THEY ARE AND HOW THEIR UNCONDITIONAL LOVE ALWAYS TEACHES US ABOUT OUR HEAVENLY FATHER. GOD TELLS US THAT RIGHTEOUS PEOPLE TAKE CARE OF THEIR ANIMALS. THIS BOOK IS ABOUT THE THIRD SON IN OUR FAMILY. OUR FOREVER PUPPY, SIR DUKE BENFORD NAMED AFTER A FAMOUS COLLEGE AND FAMOUS SONG! WE HOPE THAT WHEN YOU READ THIS BOOK, YOU CAN FEEL LOVE ALL OVER!

WITH LOVE AND KINDNESS,

TONY BENFORD

WHERE'S DUKE? NO DUKE! STOP BARKING AT THE DOOR!

DUKE! IF YOU DON'T GET OUT THAT BED AND GET ON THE FLOOR!

DUKE, COME INSIDE, IT'S STARTING TO RAIN!

BOY, GET OUT THAT MUD, BEFORE YOU START MAKING STAINS!

NO DUKE! DON'T EVEN THINK ABOUT GOING IN THAT STREET!

NOPE! OUT OF THE KITCHEN, THOSE AREN'T YOUR TREATS!

Son, not on the fresh clean clothes!

DUKE! WHY ARE YOU UNDER THE BLANKET SNIFFING MY TOES?

PLEASE DON'T GO OUT THERE AND CHASE THAT CAT!

DUKE! COME OUT THE YARD BOY, IT'S TOO MANY GNATS!

IN THE TRASH DUKE? REALLY?

DUKE, YOU'RE NOT ABOUT TO CATCH THOSE BIRDS, SILLY.

DUKE, YOU DON'T HAVE TO GROWL, IT'S JUST A BONE!

BOY YOU WERE THIRSTY! YOU GONNA SIP 'TIL IT'S GONE?

THERE HE GOES AGAIN, CHARGED UP AND WIRED!

WHERE'S DUKE? THERE'S DUKE. SLEEPY AND TIRED.

YOU'RE APART OF OUR FAMILY AND WE LOVE YOU!

WHERE'S DUKE? "RUFF, RUFF!" HE LOVES US TOO!

DO YOU WANT A BELLY RUB? A PAT ON THE SHOULDER?

DEDICATED TO SIR DUKE BENFORD ♪"YOU CAN FEEL IT ALL OVER"♪

www.ingramcontent.com/pod-product-compliance
Lightning Source LLC
Chambersburg PA
CBHW041822040426
42453CB00005B/131